Saints of Little Faith

Saints of Little Faith

Megan Pinto

Four Way Books
Tribeca

For my family

Library of Congress Cataloging-in-Publication Data

Names: Pinto, Megan, author.
Title: Saints of little faith / by Megan Pinto.
Description: New York : Four Way Books, 2024.
Identifiers: LCCN 2024000665 (print) | LCCN 2024000666 (ebook) | ISBN
9781961897144 (trade paperback) | ISBN 9781961897151 (epub)
Subjects: LCGFT: Poetry.
Classification: LCC PS3616.I5797 S25 2025 (print) | LCC PS3616.I5797
(ebook) | DDC 811/.6--dc23/eng/20240125
LC record available at https://lccn.loc.gov/2024000665
LC ebook record available at https://lccn.loc.gov/2024000666

This book is manufactured in the United States of America and printed on
acid-free paper.

Four Way Books is a not-for-profit literary press. We are grateful for the assistance
we receive from individual donors, public arts agencies, and private foundations
including the New York State Council on the Arts, a state agency.

We are a proud member of the Community of Literary Magazines and Presses.

Contents

Notes

But in my arms till break of day
Let the living creature lie,
Mortal, guilty, but to me
The entirely beautiful.

- W.H. Auden, "Lullaby"

Solstice

Somewhere the lake's shore
meets the overcast dark, gulls

        teeter across the ice.

      Sometimes they slip, their boat-bodies rocking.

      Sun melts a cool
      blue pool at the center
      where two swans dive.

      Sometimes I am hungry, angry,
      lonely and tired, all at once.

I google the gulls–not seagulls, maybe a black-tailed gull. . .

      Why must we persist
      within such cold?

A woman in a down coat examines berries at the market, off-season.
They are hard like stones.
      I want to pluck
          stray feathers from the seams
          of her sleeve, return them to her hands.

I.

Genesis

God made the world with his mouth.
He spoke, and heavens appeared.

Imagine a room with no windows
or doors   (once, trapped on an elevator in Paris

                        far away from everyone who knew
                        my name, I was free to be anyone).

Even before sun, there was light–
God smiled and his teeth

gave off an ethereal glow. There are places
                      I can't go, like the deep sea, where

                      I could not watch a bathynomus
                      giganteus emit light. There are things

                      I cannot say, like how dinoflagellate
                      who fornicate, relate to dinoflagellate

who divide themselves into two.
All power is a kind of force.

My father tells me when he was a child,
he was bad. Nuns beat his wrists and slapped

his hands with sticks. Sometimes his pinkie
will not fully flex. When he recalls these days

                      I do not know what to say, but I stay
                on the phone and we breathe. He tells me:

You know, I hate hanging up the phone.
Whenever I do, I'm alone.

Original Sin

In High School I made out with a boy
who said I smelled like curry. In the woods
behind the baseball field, his hands

undid my bra. We leaned against the fence.
Afterward, I would sit in algebra and run my
fingers over my calves, where thorns

scratched. Sometimes I found blood.
Sometimes I pressed my sternum to my desk
so hard I couldn't breathe. Math willed me

into logic, but I wanted intensity. I thought
sorrow could transform me. My mother
left her mother to move to North Carolina

because she married my father. She wanted
to change her life. I wanted to be an actor
because I wanted to exist. The first time

my mother saw me act was the last. I was cast
as Juror Eleven and told to practice my Indian
accent. After the play, my mother stood without

touching me, her blushed cheeks, red. Jesus
suffered, then rose from the dead. Wasn't I, too,
blessed? Although God sees us in the dark,

even Jesus felt lost. Once, after rehearsal,
I searched my mother's closet. The assignment
was to dress in your character's best. I knew

better than to take her things but I stole
a nude lipstick and a silk blue blouse—
it had ruffles down the center, like

a kind of spine, but softer. Like something
trying to bloom.

In Heaven, There Will Be No Bodies

which exist to tempt us
and move us toward grace.

I try imagining a bodiless place, full
of holographic angels and Saints, walking
through clouds or staring
into space.
                        When I think of grace,
I see my grandmother on the carpet
folded over at her knees. I see
my mother in lamplight, eyes closed and feeling
for the next Rosary bead. As a child,

my mother waited outside St. Michael's
in Mahim, for rations of milk and curds
of cheese. She tells me they had only
white bread to eat, which is how I imagine manna,
torn and falling from God's open palms
like bags of Sara Lee before geese at the park.
Inside all my Bible picture books, God's face
is European, maybe even
Portuguese. But what's
                        in a name?

At the discount bread store, all the bread
looks the same.
Some Saturdays I wander the aisles while
my father washes our blankets at the laundromat.
I hate Raleigh, where my body stays bruised
from games at school. Only the body holds

what the mind cannot.
At my grandmother's funeral, bruises
blue her arms, and we learn these are marks
from where she was bound by the nuns
for speaking too loudly at meals.

I batter my body
to make it enslaved,
wrote Saint Paul
to the Corinthians. In high school, I study
feminism by night, religion by day.
Each morning, I spend an hour
straightening my hair and lining my eyes.
I read somewhere that one should imagine
a god as someone they can trust. The author
chose a female God, a kind of god

who radiates light

       that does not blind.

       So I close my eyes.

Coming of Age

Late autumn, and I am daydreaming in chemistry
when my teacher stops our lesson because he is sad.
His fiancée died years earlier
in a crash. I imagine an oak tree shattering
the car's black hood, and a broken
wood fence along a nameless dirt road. I remember
how my teacher's thumb pressed
against the marker's blue cap.
After class, I lay in the shade and ran
      my hands through the grass.

When I was small, my mother taught me to count
all the different shades of green I could see.
She was trying to calm me.
I count greens when I ride trains, I look
for greens on the subway–even underground
as I hurtle through the night–
like when that man put a gun to his temple on the R.

We don't always get what we want.
When I was nineteen, my boyfriend drove his car
into a tree. It was sunny, mid-afternoon.

In Brooklyn, you can bike Bedford Ave.
and pass monuments to bikers who have crashed.
Each one: a white, crumpled bike, chained
to a bus stop. It was spring when his car
veered off the road. And each new spring,
I feel an old sorrow. Everything blooming, but my heart

is an empty room, where I hoard receipts, notebooks, volumes
of encyclopedias, unused. My mother hoards, too.
When she was thirteen, her sister Vanita was given
the wrong injection for the flu. Today,
I learn Vanita means *woman* in Hindi, a language
wholly unknown to me, except
through another's translation.

How many times did my mother tell me the story
of how Aunty Vanita died?

Obsession is a godless place. I go there every day.

Parable

My father would say *if you aim for the stars,*
then you fall on the trees.
If you aim for the trees, then you fall
on the ground.

When my father came home from the store,
his white collar was brown. He would sit
with his back to the muted TV.

I wanted to be like a kid on TV and so
I invented a dog–
we took walks with a rope
I found in the neighbor's backyard.

While I waited each night for my father,
to show him the life I could build,

my mother would serve him fresh rice and dahl.
In America, he wore a red tie.

When I went to his store as a child, I would run
down the aisles to visit the lobsters near death.

My father would unbind a lobster—
the lobster would cling to his tie.

Seascapes with Father

We ride the train through Mumbai
        and I fall asleep. At Churchgate, my father
                and I sit and watch the sea.

I am seventeen and waiting to become.
        The whole plane ride over, I flip
                through glossy college catalogs

stare at the green expanse of campus
        lawns and red gold maple leaves: a perfect
                East Coast fall. I am trying to imagine

my new life when I am returned
        to the place of my parents' birth. I tell
                my father that the beach in Mumbai

reminds me of Miami, where we drank
        from coconuts through straws. In Miami,
                my father showed me how to cleave meat

from the coconut and we licked juice
        from our palms. By the time I leave
                for college, my father will not speak to me.

Years later, when I call my father
    from New York, I will walk to the East River
        and show him my view of the city. Through our phones

we will look at each other, and the estuary,
    and maybe I will tell him how once, in college,
        I tried to write down everything I knew of his life

and only filled a page.

Anonymous City

Little fire, small flame. He tugs at the belt loop of my jeans. We let our bodies sway. I live in a dining room above a busy street, a naked bulb dangling over me, my futon, my mismatched sheets—I am love's reckless student. I take copious notes. Listening to my roommate and her boyfriend fuck, I would open my window if I had one. But in a hotel bar, beneath my hotel room, I could be anyone. I say things to my bartender like *you missed me,* and we laugh and take shots. In hotels, I rest soundly, eating pre-packaged snacks, drinking small bottles of wine. All my life, I wanted to be close. Closeness, a dance the Hudson makes with the shore. I waitress at a seaside cafe–the kind where my manager applies more blush to my face, sharpens a red pencil for my smile. When I left home, wanting only nights where the night didn't end, to pass among bodies in the dark, to feel the love of sleepless hands. . .

It's 4:00 a.m. on the Q train when a man shows me his dick.
The cover of night is sleep. To be awake
is to be seen. I ball my fists
into my chest.

        O my heart, my dove!

                Who will love

                      you forever as you are?

The Unfolding

I let a boy lick my paper skin because he told me I was pretty.
I let a man undress me because he wouldn't stop kissing me.
I left my body at a party, and then I left it again.
A secret: sadness has no sound. Like how
at 5:00 a.m. I awoke in the back of a cab somewhere
        in Brooklyn, the driver watching me.

I learned to love with nobody watching.
In my carpeted room, I was small. While outside,
tall trees blocked out a blinding sun. God moves
in the laying on of hands—a child shivers in a church,
her body wet with water. Then someone holds her, warms her,
        blesses her. I miss Raleigh in the winter,

I miss Ohio when it rains. In college, I would drive out
past the fields, down the empty highways, two lanes flagged
with fences, cows ambling, sun setting, sky growing pink.
A secret: I let a man undress me because he wouldn't stop
kissing me, and though I found him to be beautiful, my mind moved
        to light shifting among trees, fields unfolding.

Tonight, It Is Snowing in Rome

is a line that I wrote in my notebook
inside my hotel in Prague, where a woman I did not know
slept next to me, and outside the world slept, too.

Snow fell down on the cobblestone streets.
Some part of me was on alert, but I told myself
there is no danger here.

Each morning in Prague, I woke up
and ate hard-boiled eggs with ham and tomatoes with bread
and butter and jam. I warmed my sweater
over the heater while I braided my hair. Who was I
to be anywhere? Walking along the Vltava

I was cold but still alive.
Back at college, my life had become something else.
When my boyfriend would shove me, I
would sometimes cry, but only
when he could not see me.

I boarded a plane to Prague because my school
gave me a list of cities, and I picked a beautiful one.
Laying in the hotel's narrow twin bed, I closed
my eyes. Before my grandmother died

there were signs. In Prague, the story I replayed
was from Mumbai: my grandmother bent over to get something
from the fridge, when she heard her caretaker unbuckle
his belt and unzip his pants, his waist closing in.

     How should I prepare for all
     the things I cannot see?

     In Prague, I was supposed to develop
     my voice. Instead, I watched a lot of plays. There was
     one: a dark comedy where a woman is raped.
     The actor grabbed the actress by her armpits and swung
     so fast her legs took flight. She made contact
     with the wall.

I don't remember the rest of the play
just like I don't remember the last thing
my grandmother said to me, but maybe
it had something to do with my studies, or the eventual
Good Man her prayers would lead me
to marry, or maybe she just asked me to pray.

Confession

I used to have a boyfriend who would count

                my calories and refuse to kiss me
                if I finished the food on my plate

I used to study the mannerisms of other girls

                how they laughed or brushed stray hairs
                off their faces when they smiled

In middle school I loved a boy

                who did not see me   My tongue
                grew heavy with lead

I used to read his horoscope

                and mine in bed, willing our love
                to be written in the stars

Across the landscape

                of the cosmos   angels stutter
                and Saints fall

How many times have I bartered with God

                for love over my life
                They say addiction is a spiritual disease

Walking along the Hudson

                damp with sweat   I am back in
                childhood kneeling
                by the window   waiting for my
                father to come home

Love educates

                the imagination Even back then
                I wanted   to see God's face

I remember closing my eyes so tight

                I saw stars   The wood
                left marks on my skin

Summer of Nectar and Green

I plucked a honeysuckle when I wanted
something sweet. My mother cut my hair,
told me not to leave
the porch, which is why
I was running through a stranger's backyard,
when it was nearing dark, when I tumbled
into a metal latch
that held the gate shut.
                              Later,
I held napkins to my shoulder, watched each one
burst: red.

My skin would take days to purple and blue. Each day
I nursed my wound in the bathroom.
Call it childhood, but under those lights,
I was cleaning a gunshot crater
from a saloon shoot-out, healing
the deep slice of a dagger, turned upon me,
as I battled that zombie through the night. . .

                              *

    It was only after she died
that I learned my cousin's husband locked her

24

in the bathroom for days at a time. I wonder
what she bartered with,

against the God of her mind.
Here's a sad story that I'm not supposed to tell: When my mother
asked *why* this happened and *how* and *what God* could allow

such suffering

I had to remind her of the time
she read my diary.

Months later, she confronted me

about the fact that I had sex. She cried

and told me *everyone makes mistakes*

and when I told her *it wasn't a mistake*

she cried

like someone had died, and maybe

I died, because in that diary

that I wrote in for months, hiding out

in my dormitory, I wrote down things

I could never say, like when

he entered me, I would beg

to someone inside my mind

for him to *just* speak to me again, or how

at lunch, to keep some peace

I would undress, instead of eating

let him move his hands

over me. But all this

my mother did not notice

when she read my diary, or maybe

it was just my problem

to bare.

*

When I fantasize about the lives
of other women, goodness
is the thing I envy most.

When I join the gym
it is because I want to feel
like *them*, but also because I want

to outrun a bear (if I have to),
not that I have ever seen a bear,
but I heard one, once, in the mountains,

it's feet padding along the dirt
and trail rot, its body bumping into
a tree's thick bark—no, when I say

I want to outrun a bear, it is because
of all those times I am late
coming back to the apartment

where my boyfriend waits, and I feel
this *electricity* surge through me,
almost as if I have seen a bear, or I know

one is there, but I am alone
on the trail, far from home,
and though I search, I have nowhere

to run, and what if this time
                              he is not so kind.

Falling

Snow is falling to the earth, though here
 where I live, it is spring. Outside my window,
  a man pushes his bike across ice.
   I think I know loneliness but then
    I feel it again—sharp like a knife that enters me
     clean. I have never been stabbed, but once
      I came close: on the subway, at night, a man
       showed me his knife to tease me.
        He reached for my bag. He reached
       for my hair. I pretended he was not there,
      though I held my backpack to my chest like a shield.
    In Prague, there are no fences
   at the ends of cliffs or the tops of hills.
  Drunk at the edge of a beer garden at night,
   I let my feet dangle in the air, then my calves,
    then my thighs. It was sensational to look down
     over the Vltava, cutting through the city at night,
      lights on the castle, every small, winding street.
      I've loved men who bit me.
     My body in their mouths—how many times
    have I seen the underlayers of my skin?
   In my former life, I was an octopus. Before that,
  a priest. In this life, I ride the elevator up
and down and up again so that my body

can feel the feeling of falling.
   It's true: when you fall, the heart rises, physically
      into the throat, as if to counter the doomed
                                                body.

The Blind

Each morning in darkness, my father
readies himself to wake. He will log

yesterday's balance in a ledger, fill a bucket
with loose coins. Years ago, my father left India

drunk. He had some clothes in a bag. What
did he wish for? What did he want? I became

his daughter twice: when I realized how little
I knew of his life, and how little he knew of mine –

sleeping among strangers on a late-night train,
my heart beating steady and slow. My father

warned me the world could be cold, that people
would never understand me. Now he calls

to tell me he is losing his sight. From my street
I can see the Chrysler, Empire State, stars. Along

the East River, ships pass by at night, with names
I cannot see. Across the water, light from the city

finds me. Somehow, I must learn to live
in this world. Such an easy metaphor, light.

Earth-Like

At home, we keep my father
from the news. The news addles
his mind. Our doctor tells all her patients
to turn off their screens, to consider knitting
or meditation instead. She has experienced
the mind's slow pull
toward oblivion.

My father fears economic collapse.
He would feel more comfortable if I
would only withdraw $200,000
in cash–just to have on hand.
I thought the end would need more
bright angels in chariots, a sudden bloom
of locust in the tap water,
but no. The light each morning
is the same. When I sleep, I sleep fitfully,
each hour opening an eye to check
for the sun's slow rise
over the neighbor's lawn.

Alone, I resume a documentary
about outer space, an urgent search
for another planet just like Earth.

It's very possible, scientists say.
A PhD in Hawaii demonstrates centrifugal force
with her fire fan. On the International
Space Station, astronauts see sixteen
sunsets and sunrises in one
human day. Imagine feeling
you could begin again.

II.

Even in silence, I hear my father's voice

calling out to me. My name, a phantom, trembling the air.

I carry his jaw, his nose, the shape of his face on my face,

his name. Like my father, I have a hole I cannot fill.

My father is perseverating, moving around the edges of rooms. On repeat, he asks, *but how will we pay for it? How will we pay for it?*

He follows me, my mother, then me, then my mother. Inside my childhood home, there are only so many rooms.

On Christmas Day, I bake a loaf of frozen bread. I feed slices to my father with my hands, then catch each chewed-up bit he pushes back out with his tongue.

He is speaking.
I am numb.

At home, we keep my father from the news. The news addles his mind.

In November, Russian hackers on the news. Then my father calls with
news: our accounts have been hacked, our computer. . .

He tells me about the white car circling the cul-de-sac. Ours. Where it
parks. How it stays.

Evidence. Of plot or threat.

Because my father refuses to drink or eat, we try to feed him ice chips with a spoon.

The chips melt and pool in the pink plastic bowl we hold under his chin, as he turns his face from side to side. Was I like this when I was a child?

I lean over the table to help my father stand. My heart beats in the doldrums, saying

I
can I
can I
can

In the hospital, I tug the patterned curtains closed. A man laughs in the next bed over. I cannot see his face, but I imagine round, soft cheeks. He has a kind of laugh like that, full, sent up from a belly that must protrude.

The nurse will keep the man until he sobers up. She reminds him not to drink so much. The man smiles and says *of course,* and *thank you,* and

please don't go—

I sit beside my father and watch his IV drip. Each drop of saline hydrates his veins, his dry cracked skin. Today my father weighs 107 lbs. and is too weak to stand.

I pop an earbud in his ear and keep one in mine.

We listen to love songs.

In the hallway, the doctor gives me a working diagnosis, Major Depressive Disorder with Psychotic Features.

He describes ECT treatments, the QT interval, how the brain will seize up but that doctors know how to relax the body. My father should feel no pain.

Because the door to his room is cracked, my father calls my name. He wants to know what I am saying.

I ask the psychiatrist if this will end, and when.

He smiles. Psychosis is cyclical, it crests like a wave.

I think of a storm coming over my father's body, like how rain floods the neighborhood pool in the summer.

All that displaced water.

On my phone, I watch a video about a chicken too fat to stand. It lays on its back, kicking its legs, flapping its wings. There is no avail. Oversized breasts protrude.

The other chickens do not stare. They go on, walking their circles around and around and around the cage.

My father says he wants to die. He is kept alive by IVs. Depending on his labs, a little sugar, a little saline. He will not eat for fear of what *they* have put in the food. He warns me not to eat, too.

The sitter ranks his behavior on a chart in :15 minute increments. The sitter says my father is gentle and calm. Only, he shows no inclination toward hygiene, and as I know, will not eat, or willingly move.

Alert, my father grabs my hand, and asks *what should I do?*

whatshouldIwhatshouldIwhatshouldIdo
whatshouldIwhatshouldIwhatshouldIdo
whatshouldIwhatshouldIwhatshouldIdo
whatshouldIwhatshouldIwhatshouldIdo
whatshouldIwhatshouldIwhatshouldIdo
whatshouldIwhatshouldIwhatshouldIdo
whatshouldIwhatshouldIwhatshouldIdo
whatshouldIwhatshouldIwhatshouldIdo
whatshouldIwhatshouldIwhatshouldIdo
whatshouldIwhatshouldIwhatshouldIdo
whatshouldIwhatshouldIwhatshouldIdo
whatshouldIwhatshouldIwhatshouldIdo
whatshouldIwhatshouldIwhatshouldIdo
whatshouldIwhatshouldIwhatshouldIdo
whatshouldIwhatshouldIwhatshouldIdo
whatshouldIwhatshouldIwhatshouldIdo
whatshouldIwhatshouldIwhatshouldIdo
whatshouldIwhatshouldIwhatshouldIdo

My father lifts his gown to show me his diaper.

He asks, *how can I go to work like this?*

He licks his cracked lips, the layers of skin peeling.

He pushes the dead skin back with his tongue.

When I am not at the hospital, I read novels and eat apples and listen to music with words I do not know. I am calm. Like a serial killer.

Me, buttering toast, pouring coffee, ignoring the phone–such delight.

If only a camera could pan over my morning routine, underscored by the warm sounds of Bossa Nova or Mariachi, then cut suddenly to my father's severed head, sitting on a platter in the fridge.

The vacant stare of death, and my cilantro wilting in an old jam jar.

My knife would cut into the egg's translucent skin, spilling the yoke.

O, I would wipe the plate clean with bread.

Some mornings, I consider all the men I've loved and lost.

I do this half-awake in bed. Even in my sleepy state, I cover my eyes.
Do I feel shame? Do I feel surprised?

I understand loneliness as anything physical promised, then denied.

O, heart—a new day. My eyes open to an empty room.

Some mornings, I wander barefoot into the backyard. In the spring, small animals stumble forth onto the lawn.

Once, in grade school, I found a baby bird that had fallen from its nest. I brought it water in a shallow bowl. The bird steadied itself, walking forward to wet its beak.

At school, we were taught to let nature take its course. You could not play God to every living thing. The bird had its sovereign right to thrive or die.

So did I.

Mirtazapine
Zyprexa
Lorazepam

I like the long vowel sounds of my father's medications. I recite them so I
do not forget.

MirtazapineZyprexaLorazepam.

Something for sorrow, something for pain.

How the mind searches, restless and in vain.

When my father is not perseverating, he drifts in and out of sleep. I open my book to the hallway's light, but still I cannot read.

What is love without grief?

Even my thoughts grow quiet inside this dark and windowless room.

Sometimes I give an excuse, feigning hunger (I have no hunger, I have no need), I wander the hospital halls. My fingers trace bubbles in the paint.

When the mind is haunted, the mind is stalled.

There is a particular sort of sorrow I reserve for these nights. I sleep in my childhood bed. I care for my parents.

At night, I consider how I've always loved blue. So much love–I painted all my walls. The old mobile casts shadows of stars and crescent moons.

In honor of the person I used to be, I listen to the same sad songs (Snow Patrol's "Eyes Open," "Chasing Cars". . .) and–why not?–I paint my nails mint green.

My God, My God
why have you forsaken me?

Growing up, I was a Little Prophet of the heart's unrest.

Each night before bed, I imagined a new way my father could crash the car, and how my mother would flee forever, this time through the backyard.

I imagined disaster in so many ways—tripping with scissors and stabbing an eye, a gnarled fish bone slicing my throat, blood sputtering as I gasped and choked.

The mind, approaching rest, hesitates.

Some nights I call my father on the phone, and we rehearse our well-worn roles:

Are you eating?

                        A little.

Why not?

                        It's difficult. . . to explain. . .

.

.

.

Do the nurses give you water?

                        It's here.

Can you try to drink some?

                        I'll try.

.

.

.

How's your roommate?

                        I don't know.

What's his name?

                        I don't know.

Is he nice?

.

On the radio, Adam, from Nashville, is halfway through his Great Couch Tour.

Through his phone, he records the songs he writes. People online send him money to pay for his son's medical bills. Already two, and the bones of his son's small hands have fused.

The father writes love songs. What else is there?

My mother texts me from the next room over to tell me that she misses my father.

She says my father's illness reminds her of her mother. Cut off from the people she knew, my grandmother died alone.

My mother bursts into tears at some unspecified time each day, but usually in the evening, occupied by some mundane tasks, like washing dishes or boiling water for tea. Each night, she will send me a text, describing her grief.

Sorrow is a circle; it moves like the sea.

At night, I stare into the dark, and darkness stares into me.

Consider the separation of church and state, of soul and body. No more evident than inside the hospital.

While hooked up to an IV, getting an intramuscular injection of antipsychotics, my father can watch advertisements for mattresses, prescription drugs. Late at night, there are so many concerned attorneys, greasy fast-food smiles, and friendly automotive dealers who want to make you feel like family.

O, the mind, a star flung out from the galaxy, lost to the vastness of space.

My father always wanted me to become a doctor.

In the hospital, beside my father, I close my eyes.

I imagine myself in a white lab coat, a stethoscope thudding against my breast.

Behind each closed door, I could listen to the fluttering heart, beating inside each patient's chest.

In Raleigh, they separate the psychiatric hospital from the medical hospital. At both, my father refuses to eat. So, he grows weak.

He says it would be better to die than live like this. (107 lbs. and still he refuses to eat.)

Weak and then stable, stable, then weak. From hospital to hospital, he is shuttled back and forth across the grass divide.

Each time my father ends up in the emergency room, we repeat: a new nurse will pull the curtains shut, as my father calls my name through the pale, green sheet. The new nurse will ask me when this began and how long, and why my father will not eat.

Repetition is the rhythm of our grief.

When I go home, I will not sleep. I'll replay the day in my mind. I'll look closely for every missed sign.

Sometimes it's as if consciousness moves through me like rain.

Each day, I practice diligence in the face of despair. I open my news app, sip my coffee. I read about extreme weather. Ice storms, high tides, relentless heat.

They say insanity is doing the same thing and expecting relief.

Each day, my mother and I bring food, and still, he will not eat. I go home to read and read:
The world is wild! But it tries to persist.

Light moves in degrees of intensity, here. Birds stumble in the detritus.

III.

New Year

Each time the water returns
it has changed. I study the water's remains
dredging my soft-soled shoes.

My hair has been falling out
for months. *Shame, shame* replaces
my name, a familiar pull toward lament.

I pore over my blood work. Sun
breaks over my shoulder, a pothos rooting
in an old olive jar.
                    The Buddhists say *when*

we die, it will feel as if we are waking
from a long and troubled sleep. I touch
my scalp, willing it. Winter passed

before it came–snowless walks, bare streets.
Alone, I am stilled by the lake's edge, where
wind sways the reeds and used condoms drift

by my feet.
            Into the expanse of lake

I practice picking up a thought

then throwing it away.

It Was the Winter of My Life

Afternoons, I watched light fade
from brownstones. I took
long, aimless walks by the water. Each day
more leaves fell. The starkness
of trees, their sheer nakedness. . .

My friend called to tell me about a neighbor
who cornered her in the stairwell
and kissed her. She described
standing perfectly still.

The shape of the lake nearing dusk,
its symmetrical, man-made enclosures.

Rumi speaks of sorrow as a clearing
of leaves, making space for joy. But what
to do with rage? And in such a desolate
landscape?

Walking to my car from the library, a stack of books piled high in front of
me, I was stopped by a parked SUV, filled with laughing men. They had
parked in front of my—how did they know?—car. They looked at me and
laughed uproariously and continued to laugh as the man in the driver's

seat got out. I don't remember what I said, but I used the word *please.*

Consider the accrual of knowledge. There are facts, like the mechanics of throwing a punch, how abdominals contract, twisting the torso, powering the shoulder, arm extending, knuckles
bursting skin, such force(!), a fire from within.

My friend says you go through life thinking
you're a person, then learning
people see you as an object.
A *thing* that placates
                or slakes.

                                I quiet my mind with the sight of the lake.

Trauma is not the event itself, but the body's learned response. When identifying domestic violence, professionals look for signs like a fist through a wall, a chair with three legs instead of four, the message being:
next time
                        this could be you
                                        the *you*
                being *me*, when *I* circled 37 out of 50 *Red Flags*

on the **STOP DOMESTIC VIOLENCE** pamphlet
when I dialed the 1-800 number.

In therapy, I study my enclosures, the small, dark spaces of my mind.

I practice telling myself, *you are not your thoughts,*
but the watcher of your thoughts.
The watcher, watching over you.

And then, there is the relationship
to one's own authority.
You have to decide you'll win, says a man
at the boxing ring, wrapping his hands.

Each time I spar, I choke.

Adolescence

Arm in arm, we circled the soccer field after lunch. The field was like a shallow bowl, the earth around curving up and away. *Glaciers*, we speculated. And, soon after, *what would sex feel like?* We had run through the field all morning, our mud-stained gym shorts, now a dull emerald green. My lips were so sticky with gloss, each time the wind blew, my hair would get caught. I remember the feeling of circling, one foot treading flat ground, the other keeping balance on the slope, pushing harder so I did not fall. We were so close. Trading CDs, books, scraps of wastepaper with intimate notes: *did he call you? Is your mom being quiet again?* Another time I found you in the bathroom, bruised in the face and the arm. Your dad had beat you, hard. I cradled your head in my lap, brushed the hair from your eyes. Then, I told all the teachers we had. Weeks later, nothing changed.

Tunneling

A teenage girl clutching fistfuls
of lavender on the A train—I look to her
for escape: a man is yelling

        and we are trapped by a crossing
        train.

                A familiar lurch in my chest
            tells me I have only known restlessness.

My first experience of language was
of being blanketed, it softened
wailing into song.

        I learned to listen for music
        in ordinary speech.

            (See how I make meaning
            of rage?)

That I have tried to ruin my body (in almost)
every way, but still,
it holds me...

        No. Not tried, maybe
            allowed...

I walk underground through the city, the smell
of burnt coffee enters me, somehow,

through my closed mouth.
                         Tiles clatter beneath
                         my hard soled shoes.
                                              Some violence is casual
                                            like rain.

At lunch, I eat my tuna sandwich
in the cold, a stray lemon seed
                         catching inside my throat.

Bloodshot

The doctor traces my orbital bone
with her finger, asks

> *who do you call*
> *when you're scared?*

Skin on my face, dry.
A woman passing by, tells her companion: *you know*
my brain has been damaged, I can't remember
what I've said.

I ask a shaman to retrieve the lost parts
of my soul, but the shaman says no,
that my soul is intact, just
enmeshed.

> Riding the subway, I imagine
> the man beside me, clenching
> and unclenching my throat.

The doctor says sorrow is cyclical, like seasons
of harsh rain.

> I push a pile of laundry
> to one side, the clothes

cradling my back.

People always say *you'll know love when you find it...*

But how can I describe my God-
sized hole, how
it widens
with each breath.

Faith

O perilous night, O
        darkening sky:

You smell coffee, and the skin below your blouse   burns.
You know you've hit rock bottom when
it's Friday night, again,
and here you are, in a church basement, holding tight a stranger's hand
.

In your new life, you say things like *Hi, my name is*   and
thank you for your   and
what I'm trying to say is   and. . .

You've always been a good student. You recite the 12 steps under your
breath.

Outside, it is night: lights flood the sky, the stars
tonight are just thumbtacks. You pinned
small notes to your fridge reminding you
to do this,
      that,
          stop
              searching out the eyes

of strange men in the street.

You like the women's groups best.
(In the women's groups, you think about sex less.)

It was an angel who struck the dagger
from Abraham's hand, and you imagine her awash
with the kind of light that stars cast
in the jungle, like how once you slept
in a hammock

        your backpack   a pillow
        your hammock   a blanket

                  and it was enough:
                  a kind of light like that.

Tonight, you were stuck on the train between an ad
for cancer care and Klimt, peering out
at the darkening sky. Even the tortured body
was beautiful in this light, tonight
there was only the quiet, falling
snow, and a man
nearing sleep
reaching for his bagged beer can.

Kierkegaard says to love God without faith is to see
only the self, and you think of the hospital across the street.
All night, Mt. Sinai will sit quietly, its fluorescent hallways marked
by every human grief—someone
crying in a lobby chair, someone
reciting childhood prayers.

Will God draw close

if you call?

Tonight, another party. You hide in the bathroom stall. You are

thirsty, so you bring

water to your lips,

you are careful

and still, water

keeps falling through your hands.

Snowscapes

A great procession is honking across ice
where geese call out to one another before
taking off in flocks. Water makes
their landings seem soft.

Some play and others carefully place
their webbed feet down upon ice. Some amble
across the beach, they stop to prod
bottles and chicken bones frozen
along the shore.

In Raleigh, where I grew up,
snow would grace us momentarily,
like a lapse in the landscape's memory.
For a few hours, for a few days, I was betrayed
by my cotton sweatpants and tennis shoes.

All my life, I've had doubt in the spiritual sense.

In the South: a familiar poster
plastered on the walls of every
school, waiting room: a pair
of lone footprints trailing in sand.
The speaker's voice (a man) asks God

If you are with me, then where
are your feet? And God says,
Who do you think carried you
through the deep, dark waters, across
an open sea?

The nun's habits swept against the floor, collecting
dust as fine as what was falling outside.
Of the landscape, a sudden quiet. Even when birds
flocked to our gardens for nourishment.

Some say love is shapeless, but still,
we try to measure it in words, breath,
feet. Others: love is not shapeless, but
embodied—like those beams of light
where geese now rest.
Water laps the ice.

Cosmology

It's late. We're sitting
on a boat, docked.
Our waiter brings us water
and still more wine.
My date refills
my glass, asks
if I would like
to take a trip to space.
I think of last summer:
nights by the river
watching a full moon
orchestrate a swell
of tide. The dock's
spindly legs all
but disappearing
into primordial darkness.
He lights a joint.
I think of the caves
of Lascaux, where celestial
bulls are rendered
in motion, the swift
lines of their legs
thinning into ether.
No need to explain it.

He blows smoke
into my mouth.

Cityscapes

I went to see a psychic
about my broken heart.

She told me I pick men who are wounded
like me, but show pain differently,
their rage turned out instead of in.

When I played with Barbies, I often
sent them into space.
Their open-faced dollhouse made
me cry, each time I made the dolls fall
off the roof, their hard bodies clattering
back into this life.
Yes, I suffer from romantic thoughts.
Sometimes I think suffering
is the measure of my devotion.
Sometimes not.

It takes so much to feel safe
in the world. Or is that just me?
On the subway, I look
to strangers and wonder
if one of them could want me.

Then the sudden screech of metal
returns me to my thought:

Consider the undulating rhythm of the city,
each stop and start and sudden halt.
Consider the way light breaks
across the East River at dusk, where love

does not so much come to me as
move through me.

Across an Open Field

Migratory birds make their shapes—

I hold my thoughts as separate from me
so that I can see them.

That the darkness I feel
is not mine, does not belong innately to me...

That many people have chorded their sadness
around me...

Whatever that winter was,
I have made it through.

Now I stand in diminished light, walking the lake's darker edge.

Each time we return to a memory, we change it.

So, when I tell you about those nights in the jungle, sleeping
in hammocks, the sky, for once

not dulled by human light

and how the boy, next to me, kept telling me I was beautiful, reaching through the hammocks to touch my skin, and how

I could not stand it

Does language move me closer, or further away?

Back then, I clung to my own ugliness.

If I was ugly, then I could not be loved.

Each day, river water stripped my skin of dirt. I thought
it was safer to feel my shame
than it was to want.

Maybe like everything, healing has a season, dormant, but rooting.

Like how, today, my heart is full of romantic feeling, I can see
it everywhere: *love* on the faces of strangers on the train.

Each smiling softly into their phone, or gazing
past the darkness.

For so long, I picked people who could not get along,

Desire was an arrow, but now desire
is the field.

I have three choices: to drift through life
anesthetized, to soften. . .

The lake looks frozen, but it is not.

Harvest

All summer, I prayed
for clarity of sight–light falling
through leaves, a flock of starlings
before rain. . .

Of the psychic, who counseled
repeatedly, that I must become familiar
with love, so as to see its opposite
when it rushed toward me,
those fragments, its song,
linger, rising up, now
and again.

I was to let pain
drain from me like earth,
after rain.

O, obsession, that closed fist.

(Though, here again is mist,
rising off the water just
after dawn...)

Now, autumn comes early. August leaves
brown in heat. Detritus from the maple
covers the street where
a pearled wasps' nest glistens
with dew, while wasps drift
hazily in and out.

Like those figures, which cloud the edge
of memory, dissolving each time
in a kind of rain.

How should love feel, when we
receive it?

I think of those late summer walks
through the meadow and the neighboring
meadow, where I
was not longing but the one
who was longed for.

Notes

"Original Sin" references Reginald Rose's play *Twelve Angry Men*.

"The Blind" was written after Larry Levis' "Winter Stars."

The poems in Section II were written at WakeMed Hospital's Raleigh campus, between December 2020 and February 2021.

"New Year" paraphrases a line from Pema Chodron's *When Things Fall Apart*.

"It Was the Winter of My Life" is informed by my reading of *Women's Ways of Knowing: The Development of Self, Voice, and Mind*.

"Faith" references Søren Kierkegaard's *Fear and Trembling*.

"Snowscapes" references the poem (and poster) titled "Footprints in the Sand."

"Cosmology" was informed by my reading Jo Marchant's *The Human Cosmos*.

Acknowledgments

Thank you to the editors of the below publications, where some of the poems in this book first appeared (often in a different form):

Poetry Northwest, Plume, AAWW's The Margins, The Los Angeles Review, Radar, RHINO, Ploughshares, Lit 128, The Indiana Review, The Common, Smartish Pace, SWWIM, Guernica, Rivulet, Hyphen Magazine, and the *Los Angeles Review of Books.*

To the brilliant and kind team at Four Way Books: Martha Rhodes, Ryan Murphy, Hannah Matheson, and Trish Marshall, for believing in my manuscript and bringing this book into the world.

To Weihui Lu for the use of her painting, *Full Moon Night at Truro,* as my cover image. To Beowulf Sheehan for teaching me to see myself as an author.

To Neil Aitken, Nomi Stone, Annie Schumacher, Emily Lee Luan, Grace MacNair, Leigh Lucas, Sebastián H. Páramo, and Sebastian Merrill for reading earlier versions of this manuscript and offering generous feedback.

To the many confidantes, friends and mentors who have guided me to this point including: Martha Rhodes, Clita Vaz, Becky Fink, Rachel Wolff, Madison Mainwaring, Chetna Chopra, William Burnside, Leah Nieboer, J. Estanislao Lopez, Andrew Kane, Alex McWalters,

Shannon K. Winston, Kristen Hewitt, Maja Lukić, Reed Turchi,
Kate Welsh, Danielle Mužina, Kathleen Dalton, Sonja Petermann,
Jordan Jamil Ahmed, Matthew Jameson, Samuel Cheney,
James Fujinami Moore, Tyler Murray, Beth Ann Kaminkow,
Michelle Mountain, Erika Thiede Greeley, Stephanie Mareen,
Mariano Avila, Anna Amanna Jones, Jackie Amanna Jones,
and Michele Bontempo.

To Dr. David Caplan for teaching me how to read poetry and
encouraging me to think for myself.

To the many communities which have nurtured me, including the Port
Townsend Writers' Conference, the Martha's Vineyard Institute of
Creative Writing, Poets & Writers, AWP's Writer to Writer Program,
Office Hours Poetry Workshop, Storyknife, and The Peace Studio.

To Jennifer Grotz, Lauren Francis-Sharma, Jason Lamb, and
Noreen Cargill for their stewardship of the Bread Loaf Writers'
Conference, which has guided me in writing this book. To my workshop
leaders—Rick Barot, Vievee Francis, Carl Phillips, and Victoria Chang—
for challenging my drafts and shaping my poetics. And to the 2019
Waiter cohort, and my 2021, 2022, and 2023 Admin staff-scholars, for
the gift of literary community.

To Ellen Bryant Voigt and Debra Allbery, for inviting me into the MFA
Program for Writers at Warren Wilson College, which changed my life.
And to Sandra Lim, Matthew Olzmann, Marianne Boruch, Sally Keith,

and Dana Levin, for showing me how to listen to my drafts and revise.

To Seth Barden for making each day sweeter.

To my parents, James and Daphne Pinto, for filling our home with books and my heart with stories.

Thank you. This book would not be possible without the warmth and care that each of you have shown me.

Megan Pinto's poetry has appeared in the *Los Angeles Review of Books*, *Ploughshares*, *Guernica*, and elsewhere. She holds an MFA in Poetry from Warren Wilson and has received support from the Bread Loaf Writers' Conference, the Martha's Vineyard Institute of Creative Writing, Poets & Writers, and The Peace Studio. She lives in New York City.

WE ARE ALSO GRATEFUL TO THOSE INDIVIDUALS WHO
PARTICIPATED IN OUR BUILD A BOOK PROGRAM. THEY ARE:

Anonymous (14), Robert Abrams, Debra Allbery, Nancy Allen,
Michael Ansara, Kathy Aponick, Jean Ball, Sally Ball, Jill Bialosky,
Sophie Cabot Black, Laurel Blossom, Tommye Blount, Karen and
David Blumenthal, Jonathan Blunk, Lee Briccetti, Jane Martha Brox,
Mary Lou Buschi, Anthony Cappo, Carla and Steven Carlson,
Robin Rosen Chang, Liza Charlesworth, Peter Coyote, Elinor Cramer,
Kwame Dawes, Michael Anna de Armas, Brian Komei Dempster,
Renko and Stuart Dempster, Matthew DeNichilo, Rosalynde Vas Dias,
Patrick Donnelly, Charles R. Douthat, Lynn Emanuel, Blas Falconer,
Laura Fjeld, Carolyn Forché, Helen Fremont and Donna Thagard,
Debra Gitterman, Dorothy Tapper Goldman, Alison Granucci,
Elizabeth T. Gray, Jr., Naomi Guttman and Jonathan Meade,
Jeffrey Harrison, KT Herr, Carlie Hoffman, Melissa Hotchkiss,
Thomas and Autumn Howard, Catherine Hoyser, Elizabeth Jackson,
Linda Susan Jackson, Jessica Jacobs, Deborah Jonas-Walsh, Jennifer Just,
Voki Kalfayan, Maeve Kinkead, Victoria Korth, David Lee and
Jamila Trindle, Rodney Terich Leonard, Howard Levy, Owen Lewis and
Susan Ennis, Eve Linn, Matthew Lippman, Ralph and Mary Ann Lowen,
Maja Lukic, Neal Lulofs, Anthony Lyons, Ricardo Alberto Maldonado,
Trish Marshall, Donna Masini, Deborah McAlister, Carol Moldaw,
Michael and Nancy Murphy, Kimberly Nunes, Matthew Olzmann and
Vivee Francis, Veronica Patterson, Patrick Phillips, Robert Pinsky,
Megan Pinto, Kevin Prufer, Anna Duke Reach, Paula Rhodes,
Yoana Setzer, James Shalek, Soraya Shalforoosh, Peggy Shinner,
Joan Silber, Jane Simon, Debra Spark, Donna Spruijt-Metz, Arlene Stang,
Page Hill Starzinger, Catherine Stearns, Yerra Sugarman, Arthur Sze,
Laurence Tancredi, Marjorie and Lew Tesser, Peter Turchi, Connie Voisine,
Susan Walton, Martha Webster and Robert Fuentes, Calvin Wei,
Allison Benis White, Lauren Yaffe, and Rolf Yngve.